SHE SAID SHE WAS A DANCER

SHE SAID SHE WAS A DANCER

R.D. SMITHEY

DEDICATION

to the old man in his waning days

TABLE OF CONTENTS

She Said She Was A Dancer

Peckinpah

We went

to see

a Sam

Peckinpah

movie

drank

homemade

strawberry wine

that's where I

made up my mind

Steve McQueen

up on the screen

your eyes lit up

when we pulled

into that old drive-in

the frames of

Peckinpah's movie

beginning to flicker

and I've got

strawberry wine

your presence

your scent

got me drunker

quicker

than any wine

ever could

that shine

in your eyes

so easy

to make up

my mind

First Day, Winter

The heater

reeks

of burnt dust

first time

fired up

in a year

or so

it strains

to push back

the bitter cold

like two

end career

boxers

ready to give up

the game

I once liked

the cold

but I am not

the same

Age and Cold

do not agree

so I sit

and shiver

while the heater

fights the fight

for me

A Memory of Growth

The old house

had one of those

pen drawn

height markers

wish I had pried it

away from

the door frame

before the final

leaving

a record of my

growth

of the life

I'd lived in

that place and time

a physical memory

existing only now

in my mind

Junkie

I'm a junkie

my addiction

is the page

that hint

of vanilla

the older ones

get

the grain

of the page

smooth-jacketed

hard bound

creased spine

paperback

I'm a junkie

I've accepted

the fact

The Old Man Wants a Walk

The old man

wants a walk

he basks in

the sun

and squats

in the shade

to relieve himself

his eyes unseeing

his nose leads away

the scents enliven him

momentarily

memories of

puppyhood

running through

autumn leaves

he does not run now

walk is his only speed

his time grows short

even he knows

he returns to the light

and lets the sun

bake his aching bones

the leash tugs

homebound

Outside the Window Glass

I do not know

the name

of the bird

outside the

window

dancing around a labyrinthian

spider's web

I've yet to tear down

I am ignorant

of them

a failing of

mine own

I'll just call it

beauty

the cat

grey-black and lithe

slips onto

the window sill

ears back

face pressed

to the glass

he does not care

for the name

he sees only

playful prey

The Stone That Bears Your Name

I sit

on the

stone

that bears your name

pour whisky

on the ground

an old tradition

I know not

from where

it came

but still I

find it sound

I know

you are not here

not really

just a browning

patch of ground

for which

someday

we are all

bound

it is not

the dying

to blame

it is the living

that tears

us

down

Incoming

Incoming
homebound
back where my
blood has spilled
where my feet
walked
the open fields
and stood doused
in moonlight
shining down
diaphanous and bright
cool summer wind
grazing my face
incoming, Homebound
I'm coming home today
this day I come to stay

A Bone to Pick with the Sun

I take issue

with sunsets

and dying

of the light

the colors dim

to dark of night

I take issue

with sunrises

putting paid

to the pitch-night

I grow accustomed

to one

just to watch

it lose the fight

Death, Accidental

Bug hits my windshield

dead

not like I meant to

just one of those things

maybe it's in a better place

maybe someday

we'll all be some place better

something better

you know science says

energy is neither

created nor destroyed

I quite like

that bit of knowledge

it seems to draw

everything

together for me

The Cure for Innocence

I think

this too

shall pass

but it won't be quick

it won't be easy

life has a way

of making sure

the pain lasts

of making

sure

the lessons

learned

that the

innocence

is cured

The Unknown Witness

Unknown witness

I see your eyes

you've seen

the tears

only I know

I've cried

unknown witness

I've heard your lies

you've heard the lines

only I know I've tried

unknown witness

I've seen

your smiles

you've seen the frowns

hidden behind mine

unknown witness

I've seen your time

wind down

you've seen

my will ground down

unknown witness

I've watched your life

you've seen to who

I pay the bribes

unknown witness

you've watched

my life

I've listened

to you

when things got quiet

unknown witness

one of these nights

I'll take your hand

you'll take mine

together

we'll step

out of line

out of time

out of mind

The Block

Why don't

the words

come anymore

like they

used to

do from

mind to

hand to

pen

I'm Off

I'm off
to kill
the man
who killed me
the broken things
and the pain
he willed me
an unwanted inheritance
I'd gladly return
I'm off
to kill
the man who killed me
to give him
what due
he's earned
shame

I didn't need

the seven years

luck

I don't want it

but it's mine

and mine alone

I'm off to kill

the man who killed me

I'm off to kill

I'm off

Waking/Dream

I'm awake

and dreaming

real world

can't be like this

shouldn't be like this

shouldn't be able

to see the fractures

of a mirror crack'd

of what is or

what should be

I'll just lay

and awake

I pray

when

the falling sensation

subsides

After the Fall

After the fall

after the thrill

when everything

has slipped away

and you've run out of

things to say

you don't know

how you got here

or who paid your way

all alone

at the edge

of the world

standing at

the rim

and looking down

seeing yourself

speaking

but not making

a sound

just replayed

muted memories

all that's left

behind

after the thrill

is gone

after the fall

has come

Waiting on the Wind

I hear the wind

howling like

madmen and old dogs

hear the claws

scrape at the windows

at least

that's what I

imagine them

to be

I walk

these halls

dust rising

with each step

as if the place

were breathing

alive it has

always seemed so

to me

we both

groan and bitch more

with each passing year

waiting for the wind

to push one of us clear

over the finish

waiting out a game

of odds

choking out

dust filled breaths

listening to

the maddening howl

Throwing Things

Well

I threw bodies

at the bullets

until the bodies

ran out

I threw logic

at the believer

until he began

to doubt

I threw water

at the fire

but it didn't

put it out

I threw silence

at the world

but all it did

was shout

I threw myself

off the edge

thinking I would

bounce

hey, I've been

wrong before

so why stop now?

Chasing

I've chased

in my life

too many

dragons

so many

run down

with reckless

abandon

arrow-pierced

cracked and broken

forms

littering

the lanes

I've travelled

woven between

the bodies

overshadowing

the things

that mattered

Zombie

I try

to think

of it

less and less

this nagging

dragging

the corpses

of thought

from their

graves

rotten fingers

of worry scrabbling

fetid breath

seeping through

rotten teeth

whispering

don't be brave

don't save

yourself

let the curtain fall

become

the worries

slave

Vices, Many

The vices

I've let take

me over time

are many

and wondrous

but I will

pay the price

somewhere

down the line

for the things

I've done

the ways

I've spent my time

my vices

are wondrous

and far from few

but they've helped make

what I've come to be

help build

the man you see

I wouldn't trade

a single

one

Tip of My Tongue

They may be short

they may be long

they may be phrased

slightly wrong

but they still must be

said

written

carved

or sung

they must be wrung

from our lips

if wrung

they need be

some must be

fought

to be birthed

Artifacts

I dig deep

brushing away

the age old soil

the artifacts of youth

begin to appear

I loved them then

I remember them fondly

still

artifacts of

days gone by

snippets of song

once held dear

now half remembered

friends long gone

and loves

no longer here

broken childhood things

un-discarded

kept for nostalgia's sake

artifacts of a life

perhaps more

well-lived

than I thought

A Moment of Quiet Reflection

I thought

I had been

many things

but in reflection

I have been

quite few

a sad

realization

at my age

We Were

We were dead

before

the curtain

hit the floor

we were corpse

before

the slamming door

we were nothing

trying to be more

we were yesterday

trying not to be before

we were…

Well, we were something

or other

what

I'm not

quite sure

I'll figure it out

and get

back to you

Hesitation

I hesitate
to finish it
if I do
it will be
over
ended
forever
the joy
of the journey
broken by
the flat sadness
of the destination
destinations
are always dull
overrated things

A Failing of Mine

I do this thing

where I don't

let people in

I drive them away

unintentional

but all the same

a few slip

through the cracks

cherished

wisps and rays

of light

I want to

get lost in

those moments

those like

a warm bed

under covers

they do not

know all they

mean

Only So-High

Only so-high

I was

when my

grandfather

gave me a gun

a .22

that belonged

to his father

dark patinated

bolt action

single shot

I still have

the gun

but my grandfather is gone

I was only so-high

that first time

up among the kites

and the clouds

she offered me

another toke

might as well

I figured

go for broke

only so-high

I was

the Beatles

playing low

a kiss

a touch

a glow

later a goodbye

cold as snow

it hurts

being so-high

to fall

so low

only so-high

the pills

that keep me going

changing

the world's flow

I'll be

only so-high

until they

lay me low

Whiskey Wisdom

Whiskey wisdom

bottle on a shelf

back from the mirror

I see myself

mistaken I am

It's someone else

our mouths move

simultaneously

out pours

the whiskey wisdom

words only said

with a loosened tongue

truer than blue

quicker than a gun

fighter's draw

the chill inside

begins to thaw

the words begin

to roll and fall

and slur

the world begins

to rock and blur

I will have forgotten

the wisdom

the whiskey gave

by dawn

some things are not meant

to know

some not meant to be

remembered

She Said She Was a Dancer

She said

she was a

dancer

and asked me

what I might be

I said I

was the

opposite

dancing had never

been very kind to me

she smiled

and called me a liar

dancing was

whatever I

made it to be

she placed my

hand in hers

and said she'd show

me what I had

failed to see

maybe

failure isn't all

it's cracked up

to be

Even Darkness

Even the darkness

is worth the

passing through

it often leads

to the light

sometimes

it's a train

headlight

bright, blinding

sometimes it's

the sun

warm and inviting

sometimes

it's the last flicker

of a mind

deciding

to let it

all go

to let

the light recede

to let the dark

conduct the

show

Before the Flood

Waterfall

clear, cold

downpour

rising high

we were

drowning

before the flood

neck deep

in unpaid bills

I'd burn them

for warmth

if I could

afford a match

It's cold

in here

the door

won't latch

the puddles grow deeper

around my feet

too many holes

in this

old tin roof

too few pots

to catch the rain

we were drowning

before the flood

we'll be drowning

when the flood

abates

See Me Through

All I want

is enough

enough to pay

the debts I owe

to stock the fridge

and keep the lights a'glow

all I want

is enough

for a glass of wine

on a cool

Friday night

a glass of Jack

every now and then

when I'm feeling tight

maybe I drink too much

or maybe I drink

not enough

all I want

is enough

to keep

my old bones warm

when the deep south

winter sets in

enough to keep me cool

when the sun

decides to shine again

all I want

is enough

enough

of you

to see me

through

when the dark

sticks like glue

enough of you

to draw

the warm colors

from the blue

Remember Well

I remember well

that winter smell

wood smoke

and snow

anywhere bound

we'd wrap up

to go

I remember well

that winter feel

bare skin

chapped

from cold

an invigorating

burn

any delight

in it

lost to childhood

I remember well

that simpler time

of youth

lost

only remaining real

in my mind

winter is different now

as am I

perhaps that is why

the smell of

smoke and snow

is no longer

fair and fine

Did You Hear

Did you hear

about the dead kid?

No which one?

The one who found his

daddy's gun

The three year old?

Yeah that's the one

It was Bobby's son

Poor kid

Bet his daddy

feels pretty dumb

if he still feels

anything at all

if he's not numb

with shock

If only he

hadn't left it in reach

If only he put

it up high

or behind lock and key

If only

doesn't matter much now

thoughts and prayers

won't bring him back

If only…if only

The Place To Be

This is

the place to be

Saturday nights

we live for these

a blooming flower

from a week's worth

of seeds

this is the place to be

to get high

to get low

to get laid

to bleed

to the bartender

a week's worth

of deeds

to lighten

your load

until Monday morning's

weight drags

down your head

but you'll say it was

the place to be

just the price you pay

for Saturday night

for finally being free

and as for me

I'll see you there

Louis

I have never heard

before or since

a voice

like Satchmo

some sing

with gravel

in their throats

but Louis sang

with diamonds

in his gullet

his lips to horn

a golden kiss

his pot-tinted breath

a gentle

lyrical wind

no

nobody did it like him

nobody did it

like

Louis

Homesick

I was born

in Mississippi

far from a perfect place

though not as backward

as many think

I feel at home

down there

more than any place

I've roamed

It's not to everyone's taste

I know

A lot of good people

A lot of bad too

just like every

place I've known

but I've walked

where Faulkner walked

I've shopped where a

black hair-dyed

hip-shaking

boy's

mama bought

his first guitar

I've walked the ground

where a drunken shoe-salesman's

sons's life inspired

glass menageries

I've heard Wolves howl the blues

and Kings bend guitar strings

I've read of an Optimist's Daughter

and drove through the crossroads

where a man sold his soul

and I've seen the monuments

to men and women

who only asked

for the freedom

that most take

for granted

it is far from perfect

but it is home

Kindness of the Night

I breathe deep

the air

of a

porch swing sitting

kind of night

firefly glow

cricket song

kind of night

coming rain

scent on the wind

kind of night

bathed in the light

of the porch

a too long gone

re-baptism

kind of night

not gonna leave

this swing

until daybreak

shines it's light

through our

sleeping eyes

kind of night

and we wake

itching from

mosquito bites

the one downside

to the

kindness of the night

Fortune

I have this

thing about

fortune cookie

fortunes

I've kept

every one I've

ever gotten

as if the lie

printed on them

just might

come true

It's strange

I know

keeping these

useless slips of paper

just an unexplainable

habit

I guess

one of many

I'm sure

Cover Your Eyes

Cover your eyes

child

this ain't fit to see

not for your eyes

not deeds like these

though done

they must be

Cover your eyes

child

you are not yet

old enough to see

not these kinds

of deeds

I pray you

never will be

hold innocence

as long as you can

kind and loose

like a bird

in your hand

something will take it

an inevitable thing

for now

child

just cover your eyes

Newborn

I broke it away

a false face

cracked then shattered

sharp pieces

flesh toned daggers

staggered by the cold

on virgin skin

wrinkles, not old

newborn

surrounded by fragments

of me of old

chipped and torn

shorn of them now

I am reborn

weathered by storms

yet

untouched, unworn

unblemished, unbruised

new yet used

old once more

with the fresh infused

old once more

with new flesh infused

old yet

newborn

The Hill

I take

the long walk

up gallows hill

I whisper to him

Is it a deal?

he grins in reply

rotted teeth

foul stench

his breath shallow

in anticipation

for my neck

to wrench

the rope pulls

taut

and retreats all thought

from a worried mind

and leaving nothing but

creak-sound

of rope and wood

grind of bone

yet I die smiling

for what I leave behind

my name they will cry

when comes the time

when the deal is fulfilled

and the fate of those

who bloodied me seals

when the truth cries out

and silence kills

Beloved

Beloved
dear
can you hear
through the haze?
locked away
a maze
inescapable
are my shouts
and whispers
and echo
flowing through
myriad ways
none which
lead to freedom
dearly, nearly

departed

away slips

the maze walls

I sigh

say goodbye

beloved

Intoxication

Intoxicated

by sad rhymes

I say farewell

to happier times

and freefall

into darker lines

ignoring all signs

saying turn back

last chance

to change

the outcome

of this journey

but I'm tired

of the light

so blinding

the path

I need to walk

the lies

I need to believe

It's cold

in the dark

but at least it's true

at least I'm free

to believe I

can be

something other

than a pawn

Intoxicated

by the saddest of rhymes

I understand

one light

is another dark

and we are all the same

shrouded in

the darkest light

we are all the same

Shades of Grace

I came upon

one day

a man and

struck up

a conversation was

It's all around us

he said

Just shades of grace

Grey, you mean

I replied

he smiled, sighed

shook his head

No, grace

he said

Just shades of some

there's even beauty

in the dead

we just never slow

enough to see

the things that matter

or listen

for things unsaid

even though they rattle

like a shout

we miss it all

all the world's about

then away he walked

this stranger

I thought on his words

and saw his meaning

I saw the grace

in even the darker things

I laughed at the world

and the way things stood

Heaven+Hell

Hell is heaven

and heaven hell

can you see

we're already there

It's all right here

pleasure + pain

hope + despair

beauty becomes

hard to behold

It's there

if you look

through another's

eyes

we are all different

yet the same

one's pleasure

another's pain

one's great loss

another's small gain

It's all in how

you see the thing

one's hell is heaven

one's heaven hell

through certain eyes

heaven + hell

in a

flesh and marrow

cell

Rare Art

A rare art

soft wretched

harmonies

spent hours

until

a surprise

grave of

midnight

joyous

strange

a rare work

of majestic

morning

light sits

quiet

impatient

divine

Slave to The Word

Slave

to the word

and wounded rhyme

held by tyrants

on a short leash

line

that's where

they will find me

when comes time

buried beneath

the weight of words

and rhyme

buried in

this self-dug

grave

of mine

Night's Song

Behind

Night's Song

grand

orchestras

play

slim dancers

sway

in time

childhood

laughter

grows and wanes

on the wind

behind

Night's Song

ghostly flowers

blossom

spirit blooms

eternity weeps

for coming too soon

dawn murmurs

a weak

but growing

tune

behind the song

Night sings

sorrows moan

unseen

charmless things

waiting

on sense

the sun

will bring

waiting on

wounded rays

to sing in the day

The Hits

Just the hits

no one

cares about

the B sides

even though

that's where

the good shit is

where the unheard shit is

When We Were Wild

The strays hide

in their dry

places

buried in the warmth

of each other

as the rain

cools the night

I envy them

in a way

sometimes I want

to go back

when we were wild

back when we could

slide through

the wood

like rain

on window panes

when we ran

uncaring

like red blood

through vein

hunting like

an untamed child

who still remembered

how it felt

back

when

we

were

wild

Tonight

Do you think

I could stay

tonight

with you

It's cold

at my place

I'm not asking

what you think

we don't

have to do

anything

sometimes you

just want to feel

the warmth

of another

to know

there's another

living

breathing

being

besides me

to know there's another

who needs

what you need

to know

there is sprouted

the same seed

inside someone

besides me

to know

you're still

sometimes seen

Echo Passing

Echo passing

low and dying

I let your

voice

envelop me

let the

waves

of wit

and laughter

warm me

I move closer

echo passing

louder and louder

drawing me

to whence

it came

Overgrown

Withered

weary

tomorrow

the grass blade

grows

just to be shorn

it screams

out pain

in scent

useless its

brethren it

tries to warn

that which

is normal

we call

overgrown

Evening, Summer

The rain has started

a light patter

before the downpour

we rise

from the lawn chairs

no true hurry

the rain

a respite

from the

solstice sun

the feast

filling our bellies

drawing us down

to sleep

beneath the sound

of a tin roof

chorus

Left Behind

A scarf

handwoven

made by a

mother

perhaps

handed down

to a daughter

or a lover

perhaps

wrapped

round a

chair back

left and forgotten

later to be

remembered

perhaps

to be recalled

Hey Dealer

Hey dealer
you got something
to make me happy?

Yeah for a little while

Hey dealer
you got something
to make me strong?

Yeah won't take long

Hey dealer
you got something
to make the music
sound right?

Yeah I'll have it tonight

Hey dealer
you got something
the make me
smooth and loose

Yeah I got something
to polish out the tight

Hey dealer
anything to remedy
these ills

Yeah I got something
to cure the blight

Hey dealer
I've got the cash

count it

if you like

Yeah all here all right

Other books by R.D. Smithey

....

Confessions of an Angry Old Youngster

....

The Man Who Held The World